apple

แอปเปิ้ล

aeppoen

pear

แพร์

phae

orange

ส้ม

som

lemon

มะนาว

manao

grapes

องุ่น

angun

strawberry

สตรอว์เบอร์รี

sot ro boe ri

watermelon

แตงโม

taengmo

coconut

มะพร้าว

maphrao

banana

กล้วย

kluai

raspberry

ราสเบอร์รี

ra saboe ri

kiwi

กีวี

kiwi

cherry

เชอร์รี

choeri

blueberry

บลูเบอร์รี
blu boe ri

plum

พลัม

phlam

peach

พีช

phicha

fig

มะเดื่อ

maduea

pineapple

สับปะรด

sapparot

mango

มะม่วง

mamuang

persimmon

ลูกพลับ

luk phlap

cauliflower

กะหล่ำดอก

kalamdok

zucchini

ซุกินี

su kini

eggplant

มะเขือ

makhuea

carrot

แครอท

khaerot

potato

มันฝรั่ง

manfarang

cabbage

กะหล่ำปลี

kalampli

tomato

มะเขือเทศ

makhueathet

spinach

ผักโขม

phakkhom

broccoli

บร็อคโคลี

brok kho li

peas

ถั่ว

thua

pumpkin

ฟักทอง

fakthong

butternut squash

ฟักทองบัตเตอร์นัท

fakthong bat toe nat

avocado

อะโวคาโด

awokhado

artichoke

อาร์ติโชค
a ti chok

mushroom

เห็ด

het

radish

หัวไชเท้า

huachaithao

garlic

กระเทียม

krathiam

onion

หัวหอม

huahom

beet

บีทรูท
bi tharut

leek

กระเทียมต้น

krathiamton

bell pepper

พริกหวาน

phrik wan

chili pepper

พริก

phrik

asparagus

หน่อไม้ฝรั่ง

nomaifarang